UNDERSTANDING MUTUAL FUNDS
Revised Edition

Read this No Nonsense Guide and discover

★ Investments that are easy to understand and easy to follow

★ How to get started investing with as little as $250

★ A way to have your money managed by experienced professionals

★ How mutual funds work and how to use them

THE NO NONSENSE LIBRARY

NO NONSENSE FINANCIAL GUIDE®

UNDERSTANDING MUTUAL FUNDS

Revised Edition

Arnold Corrigan
& Phyllis C. Kaufman

LONGMEADOW PRESS

The authors wish to thank A. Michael Lipper, President, and the Lipper organization for making available statistics on mutual fund performance as compiled and published by Lipper Analytical Services, Inc.

Understanding Mutual Funds, Revised edition
© 1984, 1987 by Arnold Corrigan and Phyllis C. Kaufman.

ISBN: 0-681-40238-5

Production services: W. S. Konecky Associates
Cover art by November and Lawrence

Printed in the United States of America

0 9 8 7 6 5 4 3 2 1

TO

Harry & Gertrude Kaufman,

with love

CONTENTS

1 · INTRODUCTION

Who Should Read *Understanding Mutual Funds*?

If you have a million dollars to invest, or even half a million, you will be welcomed at any investment advisory firm or bank trust department. You will be offered the best investment advice money can buy. However, if you have considerably less money to invest, perhaps $10,000 or $25,000, perhaps only $250 or $500, and you realize that intelligent financial planning is essential for your security and that of your family, finding an expert whom you can trust and who will have the time to devote to your account is not easy. Fortunately, there is a nearly perfect answer to this dilemma. The answer is *mutual funds*.

In a mutual fund, many small and some not-so-small investors *pool* their money into a large fund organized and managed by professionals. Each investor owns shares in the pool, according to the amount contributed. So, even if you have only $250 or $500 to invest, don't despair—you are rich enough to afford the best investment advice in town.

2 · WHAT ARE YOUR INVESTMENT GOALS?

To get the most out of a mutual fund—or anything else—
you need to be clear about what you are trying to accomplish. Since your future comfort may depend on how
wisely you invest your savings, you owe it to yourself to
think through your goals carefully.

Making Your Money Grow

Years ago, most Americans were content to leave their
savings in a bank of some sort and to accept whatever rate
of interest the bank paid. If they didn't need to spend the
interest every year, they left it in the bank so that their
money would grow. But habits and opportunities have
changed. People have become aware that there are other
ways of investing—real estate and common stocks, for
example—that can make money grow more rapidly.

Moreover, we are living in an inflationary world. The
real value of your dollars shrinks every year. If you don't
find a way to increase the number of dollars you own, you
automatically fall behind. In 1979–80, the inflation rate
exceeded 10 percent annually; there's no guarantee that it
won't return to those levels again.

Investment Risks and Rewards

Investing usually involves a trade-off between *risk* and
reward. The higher the reward you aim for, the greater the
risks are likely to be. If you invest for maximum growth,
the risks will probably be substantial. But even if you aim
simply at higher-than-average income, you will almost certainly take some risks that you should be aware of.

Is it a mistake to take any risks? Not at all. Risk is a
part of life, just as it is a part of investing. Sometimes there
are risks in choices we regard as safe. Money left in a

savings bank may seem perfectly secure, yet inflation may eat away the value of the money every year. The risk is hidden but it's there. Great opportunities may be wasted by refusing to take reasonable, moderate risks. In investing, as elsewhere, you should be clear as to what the risks are, keep them as limited as you can, and make sure that the risks are reasonable in relation to what you are trying to accomplish.

MUTUAL FUNDS—A REASONABLE RISK INVESTMENT

What has all this to do with mutual funds? Mutual funds have features that tend to keep your risks down. They certainly don't eliminate risk—that shouldn't be expected—but they are a remarkably good way of keeping your risks down to reasonable levels in relation to your investment objectives.

In addition, you will be able to find, among the many mutual funds available, several that are geared toward specific investment goals and the degree of risk that you feel comfortable in taking.

How the Purchasing Power of the Dollar Has Shrunk
(*20 years, Dec. 1966–Dec. 1986*)

	Annual Shrinkage (%)*	Real Value of Dollar
1966		$1.00
1967	3.0%	.97
1968	4.7	.92
1969	6.1	.87
1970	5.5	.83
1971	3.4	.80
1972	3.4	.78
1973	8.8	.71
1974	12.2	.63
1975	7.0	.59
1976	4.8	.56

3

WHAT ARE YOUR INVESTMENT GOALS?

(Continued)

	Annual Shrinkage (%)*	Real Value of Dollar
1977	6.8	.53
1978	9.0	.48
1979	13.3	.43
1980	12.4	.38
1981	8.9	.35
1982	3.9	.34
1983	3.8	.32
1984	4.0	.31
1985	3.8	.30
1986	1.1	.30

*Annual change in Consumer Price Index

3 · THE REAL DISTINCTION BETWEEN GROWTH AND INCOME

Mutual funds, and most other investments, are generally classified as being primarily for "growth" or primarily for "income." At first glance, the distinction seems clear: in a "growth" investment, the number of your dollars, or the amount of your investment, will (you hope) increase over time, while, in an "income" investment, current spendable money will be generated. But actually, the real difference is not that simple.

In some investments, there's a very clear line between growth and income. If you buy a house for $50,000, and rent it out to other people for $5,000 a year, then the $5,000 a year is your *income* from the investment (setting aside for the moment any taxes and other expenses you may have).

If, at the end of three years, the market value of the house has risen to $60,000, then you have had *growth* of $10,000 in the value of your investment (or a 20 percent increase in the original $50,000).

But in many investments, the distinction may be less clear. For instance, bank accounts and money market funds are thought of as pure *income* investments because you know that the number of dollars you put into these accounts will remain absolutely fixed and will earn regular *interest* or *dividends* that could be currently spendable. Still, if you don't need to spend this interest or dividends, you may choose to leave them in the account as a way of *making your money grow.*

It can also work the other way. Let's say that five years ago you bought shares of a "growth" mutual fund for $5,000. The fund has been successful, and while you have little or no *income* (as dividends) from the investment, the shares are now worth $10,000. This year you badly need extra money to spend. So you take $1,000 out of the account and leave $9,000 in. Thus this "growth" fund has also provided you with needed "income."

Inflation makes the question more complicated. Inflation has been an important problem in the United States since the mid-1960s, and no one expects the problem to go away in the near future. Because of inflation, every dollar you own is worth less in real terms every year. In the example of the bank account or money market fund we mentioned above, you may decide that you have to let your interest or dividends (your "income") accumulate in the account simply to keep the *real value* of your investment from shrinking because of inflation.

Spending and Saving

So the line between the traditional definition of "income" and "growth" may not always be clear, and the words may not always mean exactly what you think they mean. Let's talk instead about two very clear choices that you will have to make in planning and handling your investments.

The first choice is quite straightforward. To get away from the words "income" and "growth" let's say that the choice is between *spending* money from your investment account and *letting it accumulate*. If you are trying to protect your financial future in an inflationary world, the obvious choice is to spend only what you absolutely need and to let as much as you can accumulate.

Managing Your Risks

The second choice involves more thought on your part because it involves the degree of risk you are willing to take. What generally distinguishes the so-called income investments is that they are *lower-risk*. The value of your original investment—your "principal"—either holds absolutely constant (as in the bank account or money market fund) or is expected to fluctuate only moderately, while a relatively predictable amount of "income" is added to the account every year in the form of interest or dividends. The investment is *lower-risk* because its rewards are *more predictable.*

What is a "growth" investment? It may be a piece of property in a newly developing neighborhood, or a painting that you think will rise in value, or a share in a business that is growing rapidly. A "growth" mutual fund is a common stock fund that invests in shares of businesses that it thinks will rise in value substantially. Because there is no guarantee that this will happen and because the results are much less predictable, the *risks* in these investments are higher. If the investment is unsuccessful, its value may decline rather than grow, and even the growth investments that are most successful over the long term may fluctuate in value from year to year, often sharply. But many investors are willing to take these risks because *the best "growth" investments have built up people's money much faster than the best "income" investments.*

There are many mutual funds with outstanding growth records over periods of 15 or 20 years or more. They have proved their ability. They can be unpredictable and they do carry risk, but substantially less risk than most nonfund types of growth investments. They are well worth considering by anyone who is planning investments over the long term.

But if you are only comfortable with lower levels of fluctuation and more predictability, there are mutual funds for you too. We will say more about the different types of mutual funds below. But first let us explore some of the advantages that have made mutual funds such a popular type of investment.

4 · ADVANTAGES OF MUTUAL FUNDS

Professional Management

Let's backtrack for a moment. At the very beginning of this book, we pointed out that the mutual funds let even the small investor enjoy the best investment advice in town. With fund sizes ranging from a few million to several billion dollars, the funds can afford to hire the best managers in the world (called "portfolio managers" because the fund's collection of securities is its "portfolio").

Are fund managers really that good?

The answer is yes and no. Investment management is still more of an art than a science, and the professional managers, who are only human beings, range from exceptionally good to pretty poor. You have to know how to study the record and pick a good-quality fund (see Chapter 10) or you need to deal with a broker or salesperson who is knowledgeable and honest enough to help you choose.

How much difference does a good manager make? A big difference. Even in a money market fund, where the range of securities that can be bought is quite limited, a good manager will have an edge over a mediocre one. In common stock funds—the funds most suited for investors seeking long-term growth—the problems of choice multiply. In the common stock funds there are major differences in results among different managers, and the gap between the best-performing and worst-performing funds is very wide. But the best-performing common stock funds have made their shareholders' money grow, over the long term, at rates as much as 10 percent *above* the rate of inflation. Of course, the investment quality and performance of a mutual fund depends upon more than the skill of one or two portfolio managers. The funds have their own research staffs, and access to professional research and advisory services that are simply beyond reach of the average investor. And they work at it full time.

Diversification

In addition to professional management, a mutual fund gives you a second advantage that is important—that of *diversification*.

Diversification is another *advantage of scale*—an advantage, like that of professional management, arising from having your money pooled with that of thousands of other investors to create a fund that may amount to $50 or $100 million or more. With that amount of money available, the professional managers are able to spread the fund's investments over as many as 100 or 150 different securities. If any one of these securities goes sour, the effect on the fund is relatively small. On the other hand, if you are a do-it-yourself investor with your money concentrated in perhaps five or ten stocks and/or bonds, a disaster in any one of them will cut deeply into your total results. Diversification is an important advantage of scale because it *reduces risk.*

Note that the fund managers don't haphazardly buy many individual securities. They try to strike a very careful balance among different *types* of securities in the portfolio, so that the fund won't run the risk of having all its investments weighted in a single direction. In a common stock fund, the investments are likely to be diversified across a large number of different industries. In a bond fund, the managers might strike a balance between very long-term bonds (that is, bonds that won't come due for 20 or 30 years) and some intermediate-term or shorter-term bonds.

In theory, of course, you could diversify by buying many different securities for yourself. But this takes both knowledge and time. And because you would be buying and selling securities in small dollar amounts, you would find your transaction costs (primarily brokerage commissions) relatively high—perhaps distressingly high.

Quantity Trading

A fund has other *advantages of scale* because it buys and sells securities in large quantities. These include:

(a) *Lower Commissions*: Because the average fund trades in large quantities, the brokerage commission rates it pays when buying or selling stocks, bonds or other securities are only a fraction of the commission rates paid by a small investor.

(b) *Buying Power*: Quantity trading may also occasionally give a fund better buying or selling prices. And there are certain securities that can only be bought efficiently in large quantities—like certain bond issues that are typically traded in lots of $100,000 or more. Or consider U.S. Treasury bonds, which generally sell in units of at least $10,000, with the best prices available on trades of $1 million or higher.

5 · MORE ADVANTAGES OF MUTUAL FUNDS

There are other advantages of mutual funds that aren't direct advantages of scale, but that contribute to the usefulness and popularity of the funds. Among these are:

1. Liquidity.
2. Switching arrangements.
3. Convenience features and service.
4. Simplified retirement plans.
5. The "goldfish bowl" effect.
6. Simplified accounting.

Liquidity

Liquidity means that you can put your money in an investment and take it out easily, quickly and without penalty. A "liquid investment"—one with high liquidity—is an investment that is easily bought or sold.

Mutual funds are highly liquid investments. Every mutual fund will buy back ("redeem") its shares on any business day at net asset value. (The concept of "net asset value" is discussed in Chapter 9.)

There is no minimum holding time—you are free to sell once the check for your purchase has cleared. By law, the fund must pay you your money within seven days of the redemption date. The net asset value may be more or less than your original cost, depending on how the fund has performed, but you don't have to worry about whether there is a buyer in the market for your stock.

Switching

If your fund is part of a larger group with several different types of funds, you will usually be offered simplified arrangements for switching from one fund to another, should investment conditions or your goals change. Switching by telephone has become common, either at no cost or for a nominal fee. Many investors use this privilege for switching between money market funds and common stock funds. (See Chapter 18.)

Convenience and Service

Convenience and service are among the prime attractions that have helped the mutual funds grow. Your shares are generally held by the fund's shareholder servicing agent (a bank or other organization), so that you do not need to be bothered with safekeeping of certificates. (In industry terminology, you have an "open account," and you are credited with owning "unissued shares," or "book shares.") At least once a year, the agent sends you statements showing your transactions and the number of shares in your account. You can arrange to have the dividends automatically reinvested. All funds have simplified procedures for you to add money to your account whenever you wish; many have automatic investment plans under which you can authorize your own bank to send regular amounts to the fund for investment. And when you are ready to take money out, most funds offer automatic withdrawal plans under which shares are automatically redeemed to provide you with regular monthly or quarterly checks planned to meet your cash needs. Most funds have toll-free ("800") numbers, and if you need help in using these services, the people who answer the phones are surprisingly good and helpful at giving you the advice you need.

Simplified Retirement Plans

Most mutual funds offer simplified retirement plans, making it easy to invest your plan money for the long term, with all earnings plowed back into the account. The most popular plan, of course, is the IRA (Individual Retirement Account), which can be used by almost everyone who works for a living (see Chapter 20, and the No Nonsense

Financial Guide, *Understanding IRAs,* for more information). The IRA plans offered by the funds meet all tax law requirements. Most funds also have their own self-employed retirement plans ("Keogh" plans), approved by the IRS. Various other types of retirement plans also are offered by many funds.

The "Goldfish Bowl" Effect

The people who run mutual funds operate in a "goldfish bowl." On any given day, you can pick up the financial section of the newspaper and find out how your fund is doing. (To learn how to read the newspaper quotations, turn to Chapter 13.) You can also track your fund's performance and compare it to other funds through publications that analyze performance over periods ranging from one week to 20 years. (Such publications are listed in Chapter 11.) By contrast, it may be much harder to evaluate the performance of a private advisory account or brokerage account.

Another part of the "goldfish bowl" effect is the strict regulation of mutual funds by the U.S. Securities and Exchange Commission (SEC). Regulation does not prevent investment managers from making mistakes of judgment, but it does prevent them from taking deliberate advantage of their shareholders. In this respect, the SEC has been tough and effective. Brokers and investment advisers are regulated also, but not as effectively from the standpoint of the individual investor. All investments require careful watching, but with a good mutual fund you can sleep more soundly than with most.

Simplified Accounting

A final advantage of mutual funds is the convenience of owning a single security, as compared with owning 10 or 20 (or more) individual stocks or bonds. Your purchase and sale records are greatly simplified; you receive dividends from a single fund instead of dividends and/or interest from many sources. At income tax time, a blizzard of paperwork is reduced to a few simple entries. You can check the market value of your holdings at any time by simply multiplying the number of shares you own by the daily price published in many newspapers. (See Chapter 13.) No wonder many large investors prefer mutual funds as a matter of convenience.

6 · DISADVANTAGES OF MUTUAL FUNDS

Although mutual funds do a lot for the investor, they can't do everything. And there are certain needs they do not meet.

Not everyone wants professional management. Some people like to be personally involved in the choice of their investments, either alone or together with an investment adviser or stockbroker. While choosing stocks and bonds is a job best left to professionals, some amateurs have proved that they can do it successfully. Some people *enjoy* selecting and managing their own stocks so much that they wouldn't think of giving it up. Others like the pleasure and reassurance of talking to a broker or adviser regularly about their investments.

Some people believe there is extra merit in having a personal account at a brokerage firm, with their own special portfolio of securities, rather than sharing in the larger portfolio of a mutual fund. We might call this "the mystique of the separate account," and as far as the funds are concerned, we don't think it's a real disadvantage. There's a supposed attraction about having a portfolio selected specifically for you and adjusted to your personal needs and objectives. But unless your needs are quite unusual, it's probable that they can be met by a selection of the types of funds we will discuss. An interesting phenomenon of recent years is that many pension funds, which traditionally maintained separate investment accounts, have noted that their results fell short of what they could have achieved through the better mutual funds, and have begun putting their money in the funds instead.

You may want a broker or adviser for a more practical reason. Even if you learn how to pick a good stock fund, a good bond fund, a good money market fund—how do you decide how to divide your money among them?

How do you spot the times when the stocks or bonds are particularly attractive—or the times when prices are high and they may involve excessive risks? A broker or investment adviser is expected to deal with these problems. However, there are ways of solving the problem with mutual funds. You can buy "load" mutual funds with the advice of a broker (see Chapter 8), paying a commission for the broker's services. And in recent years there has been a development of advisory services that tell you not only which mutual funds to buy, but also when to buy and when to sell. (See Chapter 11.)

Mutual funds are also not the answer for the person who wants to take higher risks by concentrating money in only a few securities. Perhaps you don't *want* diversification—perhaps you want to put half of your savings in the latest computer stock. That's your privilege; but remember that one reason for the popularity of mutual funds is precisely because so many amateurs have come to grief by refusing to diversify and failing to recognize the speculative risks involved in owning just a few securities.

A minor disadvantage of mutual funds is that the expenses of running them (including the fees paid to the management organizations) reduce the income paid out to you. But the expenses are not great—typically from three-fourths of 1 percent to 1 1/4 percent of assets, or about $1 per year for every $100 you have invested. So a bond fund owning bonds that yield 12 percent annually might only pay out 11 percent to you. But the 1 percent cut in your yield seems a modest price for the advantages of having your investment professionally managed, with most of the accounting done for you.

There is one other problem with mutual funds that isn't exactly a disadvantage, but that needs to be mentioned. To put it simply: Even professionals need to be watched. Some people think that because the funds are professionally managed, they can be bought and forgotten. That isn't true. Fund managements change—or sometimes a fine manager loses his or her touch. Even if you have bought what seems to be the best fund in the world, or a fund that suits you exactly, you need to review it regularly to see if it is doing what you expect of it, and if the reasons for owning it still apply.

7 · TYPES OF MUTUAL FUNDS

There are mutual funds to match every investment goal. As we explained in Chapter 3, funds are traditionally described as being primarily for "income" or primarily for "growth." But the real distinction is largely one of risk.

Basically, all funds fall into a few major groupings:

1. Money market funds.
2. Bond funds.
3. Tax-exempt bond funds.
4. Common stock funds.
5. Balanced funds.
6. International funds.
7. Other specialized funds.

Money Market Funds

We suggest you read the No Nonsense Financial Guide, *Understanding Money Market Funds*, for a complete discussion of this very familiar type of mutual fund.

Money market funds share many of the characteristics of a bank. They are the simplest type of income fund, and they carry the lowest risk of all fund groups. They aim at maximizing safety, convenience and accessibility (liquidity). The dollars you put in the account generally remain constant without any fluctuation (a few money funds permit minor price fluctuations). Meanwhile, the fund earns income for your account based on whatever it can earn in the safest short-term investments—primarily very short-term loans to government entities, banks and major corporations.

Money market funds are for you if you are willing to forego maximum growth in order to have:

- Lowest risk.
- Safety.
- Liquidity.

Bond Funds

In a money market fund, your money is being used to make very short-term loans—loans that are repaid so soon that they are considered risk-free.

In a bond fund, your money is used to buy bonds, which means that you are making long-term loans, usually to the government (U.S. Treasury bonds) or to major corporations. Each bond carries a specific interest rate and is due to "mature," that is, to be repaid, at a specific future date. When you buy a bond coming due in a certain number of years, you are "locking in" that rate of interest for the life of the bond—which may be as long as 20 or 30 years.

This may sound like a sure thing. But as we suggested above, risks are not always what they seem, and locking in a long-term interest rate does involve a risk—even if the bond is of the absolute highest quality, such as a U.S. Treasury bond. As interest rates fluctuate, so does the market price of the bond. If interest rates rise while you own the bond, you will obviously wish that you had waited before investing, because by waiting, you could have earned a higher interest rate. Also, the change in the market will reduce the current market value of your bond. If your bond pays 10 percent interest, and if investors can now buy new bonds paying 12 percent, they obviously won't be willing to pay full price for your old bond. Of course, the opposite may happen—interest rates may drop, the current value of your bond will rise, and you will look like a person of foresight. The point is that no matter how "safe" a long-term bond may be—no matter how sure you are that you will eventually be paid off as promised—there is always the risk of price fluctuations depending on the trend of interest rates.

All of this applies equally to long-term bond *funds*, which are simply mutual funds consisting of pools of long-term bonds. At any given time, a long-term bond fund will probably give you a higher current return than a money market fund—the higher return is your reward for taking the risk of these price fluctuations. But interest rate trends are notoriously hard to predict, and unless the investor badly needs the extra return, bond funds should be bought only with caution.

Bond funds are an income-oriented, moderate-risk investment. They will probably give you a better return over the long run than money market funds, but be warned that they will decline in price when interest rates are rising. (For a selection of bond funds, see Table B at the back of this book.)

Tax-Exempt Bond Funds

There is a special type of bond fund that is deservedly popular with many investors. These are the funds that invest in tax-exempt bonds—the so-called municipal bonds or "municipals" that are issued by states and municipalities and state and local agencies. The income from these bonds is *generally exempt from federal income tax*. (The exemption doesn't always apply. For more information on tax-exempt bonds, see the No Nonsense Financial Guide, *Understanding Tax-Exempt Bonds*.)

The advantage of such bonds is simple. Say that you are in a 28 percent federal income tax bracket, and you have a choice between a U.S. Treasury bond paying 9 percent—remember that U.S. Government bonds are *not* exempt from federal income tax—and a high-grade, tax-exempt bond paying 8 percent:

	Treasury Bond	Tax-Exempt Bond
Yield before tax	9.0%	8.0%
Tax (28%)	2.5%	—
Net yield after tax	6.5%	8.0%

This type of calculation—which of course varies depending on an individual's tax bracket and the specific bonds being considered—has led great numbers of investors to municipal bonds. The tax advantage often more than compensates for the lower yield, compared with taxable bonds. Tax-exempt bond *funds* have relieved investors of the problems of buying and selling individual bond issues.

What about the price risks in municipal bonds? Here, too, as in the government and corporate bonds discussed above, current market prices will fluctuate depending on the level of interest rates. Often, yields on the bonds are high enough to give investors reasonable rewards for taking this price risk.

While the interest on municipal bonds is generally exempt from federal income taxes, it is usually *not* exempt from state and local taxes, except in the state where the bond is issued. In states such as New York and California where state income taxes are substantial, there are now specialized funds that invest only in bonds issued in that state. These funds are "double tax-exempt" or "triple tax-exempt"—exempt from federal income taxes *and* from state and local income taxes in the particular state where issued.

Like taxable bond funds, the tax-exempt bond funds are an income-oriented, moderate-risk investment. Here, too, be warned that the funds may decline in price when interest rates are rising. (For a selection of tax-exempt bond funds, see Table C at the back of this book.)

Common Stock Funds

With common stock funds, we leap to the opposite end of the investment spectrum. (We suggest you read the No Nonsense Financial Guide, *Understanding Common Stocks*, for additional information.) Risks are higher, and the value of your investment fluctuates quite sharply from month to month and even from day to day. There is no guarantee of your investment, and no assurance as to what growth the fund will achieve or what dividends (income) it will pay.

Why take these risks? Because common stock funds give you the opportunity for much *greater growth* than any other type of fund.

Here's why: Common stocks are shares of ownership in major corporations. Historically, as these corporations have grown and profited, the values of their stocks have gone up. At the same time, that portion of the corporation's profits not needed in the business can be paid out to shareholders (including the mutual funds that own shares) in the form of dividends.

Also, *over the long term the values of stocks have adjusted upward for inflation.* So stock prices have had a double-growth component: A component representing the real growth of the corporations, and an adjustment to inflation.

Over the long run, investors in common stocks have done far better, on the average, than investors in banks, money market investments, or bonds. But the short-term road can be bumpy. Common stocks are traded (bought and sold) actively on the New York Stock Exchange and several other markets. The stock of a particular company tends to fluctuate in price depending on the fortunes of its industry and the relative results of the company within the industry. In addition, the price of a stock is likely to be affected by broad swings in the economy, as well as by world affairs and psychological swings in the stock market.

The funds that own common stocks share many of these characteristics. But because a fund is diversified by owning many different stock issues, the fluctuations are milder and the risks are less. A few poorly performing stocks should not upset the performance of the whole portfolio.

There are many different types of common stock funds, classified according to the degree of risk they take:

1. "Aggressive growth" or "maximum capital gain" or "maximum capital appreciation" funds take the greatest risks in pursuit of growth. Some of them have remarkable

long-term records, but their shares are likely to suffer sharp price drops when the stock market goes down. These funds may use speculative investment techniques, and they may intentionally be *less* diversified than the average fund. Obviously, if you intend to invest in funds of this type, you should take extra care, and be willing to stay with the fund long enough to ride out possible short-term market setbacks. (See Table A at the back of this book.)

2. "Growth" or "long-term growth" funds tend to be a notch lower on the risk scale and their shares may fluctuate somewhat less sharply in price than those classified as "aggressive growth." In this group, too, the best funds have very impressive long-term growth records. Generally, these funds put less emphasis on aggressive trading techniques and more emphasis on investing in companies expected to show better-than-average, long-run growth trends. The quality of research is a key factor. It's worth noting that if companies grow successfully, their ability to pay dividends also increases, so some growth funds state their objective as "long-term growth of capital and income." But the current income dividends that growth funds pay are only incidental and are likely to be small. Sometimes you will see "small company growth funds" listed as a separate category; these funds concentrate on investing in fast-growing smaller companies, and they may be somewhat more volatile than the average growth fund, though the differences generally are not great. (See Table A at the back of this book.)

3. "Growth and income" funds usually put primary emphasis on growth, but they are likely to invest in larger, more stable companies that pay dividends. These funds may show less dramatic growth but also less price volatility (price swings). For the person who has not previously invested in common stock funds, one of these middle-of-the-road funds may be a natural first choice. Although you may not be interested in receiving income dividends, you should note that they add an element of stability to the fund's total performance, since the dividends are generally much more dependable year-to-year than the hoped-for

growth in value of the fund's shares. The dividends are a relatively *predictable* element in the fund's total performance. (See Chapter 10.) If you don't need to spend the dividends, you simply instruct the fund to reinvest them automatically in additional shares, as many shareholders do. (See Table A at the back of this book.)

4. "Common stock income" funds carry discretion a step further, stressing income ahead of growth and thus further reducing risk. This policy usually involves strong concentration in the stocks of larger, dividend-paying companies; it may also mean the inclusion of some bonds and/or preferred stocks for stability and extra income. (*Preferred* stocks carry the promise of a stated dividend rate if the company's profits are adequate to pay it; *common* stocks carry no certainty as to dividends.) This category of funds is often termed "equity income" funds, or "income funds—common stock policy." (See Table A at the back of this book.)

A word of caution: in common stock funds, the quality of the management can be far more important than the fund's classification. There are a few outstanding "equity income" funds that have outperformed most of the funds in the "growth" and the "aggressive growth" groups—and with far less risk. Remember also that the lines between these various groups are far from exact, funds in adjacent groups may resemble each other greatly, and the only way to be sure of a fund's classification is to study the fund's own record and policies. (See Chapter 12.)

There are also common stock funds that only invest in certain industries, such as energy, technology, or health care. Because these funds, known as "sector" funds, are less diversified than a general common stock fund, both the rewards and risks are likely to be greater, and they should be approached only with considerable care. A particular type of sector fund is the small group of funds that invests only in gold-mining stocks—a group that often performs spectacularly when the price of gold is rising, but poorly when the gold market turns downward.

Common stock funds are for you if you are willing to

take some risks in order to achieve greater long-term growth. It's important to make up your mind about the degree of risk you feel comfortable with, and then to pick your individual fund (or funds) carefully.

Balanced Funds

The portfolio of a balanced fund includes both stocks and bonds, with the objective of reducing risk. It's a traditional form of diversification, and the policy may suit an investor who wishes to be conservative. (You can achieve much the same result and have your own "balanced" portfolio by owning both common stock funds and bond funds, picking the funds that seem best to you in each category. See Table A at the back of this book.)

International Funds

There are "international" funds that invest primarily in foreign common stocks and "global" funds that invest in a mixture of foreign and U.S. stocks, as well as a few funds that invest primarily in foreign bonds. International funds depend not only on a successful choice of foreign companies and foreign securities, but also on the value of the dollar against foreign currencies. When the dollar falls against foreign currencies on the foreign exchange markets, foreign stocks and bonds become worth more in terms of dollars, and the values of international funds are likely to rise; when the dollar rises, the funds suffer. In 1985–87, as the dollar fell against most other leading currencies, several international stock funds turned in outstanding performances.

Other Specialized Funds

There are also mutual funds with other specialized types of portfolios. We have already mentioned the common stock funds that specialize in single industries, including the gold funds. There is also a group of funds that uses *options* as part of their investment strategy. Specifically, the *option income* funds use options together with common stocks in a conservative way to add to the funds' income; the trade-off is that the fund gives up some part of its growth potential.

8 · HOW TO PICK THE RIGHT MUTUAL FUND: LOAD VS. NO-LOAD

In terms of marketing, mutual funds are divided into two basic categories: load and no-load. When you buy shares in a load fund, you pay a sales commission (load). In a no-load fund, there's no commission.

The boundary between the two groups has gotten blurred in recent years, with the introduction of new sales practices that cut across the old lines. Still, most funds fall quite clearly into one category or the other.

In load funds, you typically buy shares with the help and advice of a broker or salesperson who is compensated out of the "load." In a no-load fund, you do without the broker or salesperson; you make your own choices, based on your own research, and you then generally buy shares direct from the fund. If the fund is a "pure" no-load, you buy shares at net asset value (see Chapter 9)—your total investment goes directly into the fund, without any deduction. Brokers have no incentive to sell shares of no-load funds, but many of the no-loads advertise heavily in the hope of getting you to write or phone for their prospectuses and sales literature.

Most load funds used to charge commissions of from 7 percent to 8½ percent, but some funds have dropped their rates as buyers have become more sophisticated, and it is now common for loads to be anywhere from 4½ percent to 8½ percent.

Other Charges to Look For

Because buyers are wary of the traditional "front-end" loads or commissions—that is, commissions charged when shares are purchased—many funds have turned to other charges instead. Some funds charge a redemption fee, sometimes referred to as a "back-end load" or "contingent deferred sales charge." This may be on a sliding scale: for example, 6 percent of net asset value if you redeem in the first year, 5 percent in the second year, and so on, until there is no charge after the sixth year.

Some funds that are basically no-load now impose small redemption fees on shareholders exiting during the first six months or year. And certain no-load funds have become "low-load" funds, charging sales commissions of 2 percent or 3 percent as a way of bringing in extra money to the management organization or of giving a small incentive to brokers. Some smaller no-load funds have converted completely to load status, rather than trying to compete with the bigger no-load groups. But many "pure" no-load funds remain.

12b-1 Plans

In recent years, many funds, both load and no-load, have taken advantage of a new SEC rule (Rule 12b-1) in order to establish "12b-1 plans," under which a fund itself is permitted to pay for a certain amount of marketing expenses.

While some fund managements have used this privilege conservatively, others have carved significant amounts out of fund earnings for marketing purposes. The reason is obvious: Building the size of the fund benefits the management organization (the benefits to fund shareholders are likely to be smaller, if any). The excesses have given 12b-1 plans a bad name, and the SEC has apparently considered revising or eliminating the rule under which they are permitted.

Should you avoid a fund just because it has a 12b-1 plan? Read the footnotes to the fund's financial statements. If the annual expenses under the 12b-1 plan are no more than 0.25 percent of the fund's assets, the effect on the fund's performance is minimal. But if the expenses have been high enough to be a drag on the fund's performance, look for another fund.

Are No-Load Funds Worth the Trouble?

Is it worth doing your homework and research in order to select no-load funds intelligently? Actually, if you have the inclination, tracking the funds and selecting the ones that are right for you can be *fun*. And it does make a difference. See what happens, in the following table, to two investments of $1,000 each in two funds that both achieve an identical 12 percent average growth rate. But while one fund is no-load, the other charges an 8.5 percent load—so that $85 of the $1,000 goes to the sales organization, and only $915 is actually invested for you:

	No-Load	Load	Difference
Initial Investment	$ 1,000	$ 1,000	$ 0
Initial Value	1,000	915	85
*Value of Investment**			
after:			
1 year	1,120	1,025	95
5 years	1,762	1,613	149
10 years	3,106	2,842	264
20 years	9,646	8,826	820
30 years	29,960	27,413	2,547

*Assuming reinvestment of all distributions and total growth rate of 12 percent annually.

Note that the load charge is often lower in percentage terms when you invest a large amount—say above $10,000—and you can receive this reduced rate if you make smaller purchases during the year that total the required amount.

On the other hand, you should be aware that the commission is really higher in percentage terms than the industry says. The example in the table above shows what the load funds call an 8.5 percent load. But since the net price of the shares without commission is actually $915, the commission would be calculated in most sales situations as $85/915, or 9.3 percent.

So there is reason to learn how to pick no-load funds for yourself. In Chapter 10 we will begin to discuss how to go about it.

How Do No-Load Funds Make Money?

If the no-loads don't charge a commission, how do they make their money? The answer is that the managers of *all* funds—load and no-load—charge the fund an advisory fee to cover their management expenses. This fee is one of the regular annual expenses of the fund, and has nothing to do with the sales commission. The sales commission (load), if there is one, goes to pay the salesperson or broker and the sales organization. The no-loads don't have salespersons or elaborate sales organizations, and generally finance their selling effort out of the advisory fee.

Which Is Better—Load or No-Load?

Are load funds better than no-loads? The load fund industry used to claim that they were—arguing, in effect, that you can't get something for nothing. But it's been well demonstrated that sales charges have nothing to do with management skills and investment performance. The two groups of funds have, on the average, performed about the same. There are load funds with records ranging from excellent to poor, and there are no-loads with records ranging from excellent to poor.

Why Buy a Load Fund?

Investors' needs may differ—just as some consumers buy gasoline at self-service pumps, while others are willing to pay extra for the same gasoline in order to get full service.

Selecting mutual funds takes thought and consideration. How much current income do you need? What degree of risk do you wish to take to make your money grow? Do you worry when the price of your fund fluctuates? How much stability do you need to sleep well at night? If you find it difficult to answer these questions, you may have reason to consult with an experienced broker or salesperson. And if you don't have the aptitude or inclination to select mutual funds yourself—or perhaps you simply don't have the time—a salesperson or broker who is knowledgeable and conscientious may more than earn his/her commission.

Let's say that you are baffled by mutual fund statistics and prospectuses, and that a salesperson or broker helps you pick a good fund with an 8.5 percent load that, over the years, achieves a performance rate that averages 3 percent better annually than the no-load fund you might have picked for yourself. In this case the load fund will make up the difference in value in a little more than three years, and over longer periods it will build up an impressive lead. Moral: Over longer periods an outstanding fund will outperform a mediocre fund, irrespective of load.

Finding the right salesperson may not be easy, and you should look hard for one who is not only experienced, but who is likely to be impartial where choice of funds is concerned. Many of the larger brokerage firms now sponsor their own mutual funds, which they are likely to recommend to investors. Some of these funds have had good performance records. Still, a broker whose firm does *not* sponsor its own funds may be in a better position to give you impartial advice.

9 · NET ASSET VALUE

At this point you need to know how the price of a mutual fund share is calculated.

Basically, every afternoon the mutual fund adds up the market values of securities (stocks, bonds, etc.) it owns. (For example, if the fund owns 10,000 shares of common stock of General Motors, and General Motors finished trading or "closed" at a price of $65 per share, the calculation is simply 10,000 × $65 = $650,000. And so on.) The fund also adds in the value of its other assets—its cash and any amounts it is owed. From the total it subtracts any liabilities—amounts that it owes to others for various fees and other expenses, etc. The result is the "total net assets" of the fund. This figure is then divided by the "shares outstanding" (the total number of shares held by shareholders) to arrive at the "net asset value per share," which is each share's proportionate interest in the fund's total net assets.

Obviously, if the market value of the securities the fund owns goes up, the net asset value per share will go up. And vice-versa.

On any given day, the investors who wish to put money in the fund do it by buying new shares from the fund at the net asset value calculated at the end of that day—sometimes plus a commission, sometimes not. (See Chapter 8.) The investors who take money out of the fund do it by "redeeming" shares—selling them back to the fund—also at the day's net asset value. (Note: A few funds impose a charge on redemptions. See Chapter 18.)

Incidentally, this means that you never know at exactly what price your order for purchase or redemption will be executed. All orders received by the fund on a given day before the close of trading are executed at whatever price is calculated that day, which can only be done after the close.

Money market funds are an exception. Most money market funds make a practice of holding their share values constant—usually at $1.00 per share—and they own securities that ordinarily show only fractional variations in market value.

The mutual fund pricing structure is honest and straightforward and works well for the shareholder. What you see is what you get.

10 · EVALUATING PERFORMANCE

Before you can choose a mutual fund intelligently, you need to know how the performance of different funds is compared.

There are three ways a mutual fund can benefit its shareholders.

1. Payment of dividends.
2. Payment of capital gains distributions.
3. Increase in net asset value.

Payment of Dividends

During the year most funds earn "investment income"—dividends on the stocks the fund owns and/or interest on the bonds and other fixed-income securities it owns. After deducting expenses, including the management fee, what is left is "net investment income." On some schedule—monthly, quarterly, annually, or other—the fund pays this net investment income to shareholders as "income dividends." Each shareholder receives dividends in proportion to the number of shares owned.

Payment of Capital Gains Distributions

The fund may also "realize" capital gains—i.e., make profits for its shareholders—by selling securities for *more than* the fund paid for them. At the end of the year, if these capital *gains* outweigh any capital *losses* (i.e., from the sale of securities at *less than* the fund paid for them), the difference or "net gain" is ordinarily paid out to the shareholders as a capital gains distribution. By law, such a distribution can only be made once or twice a year.

Increase in Net Asset Value

If the securities in the fund's portfolio rise in price, on the average, then the net asset value of the fund's shares also will rise (see Chapter 9), and the shareholder's investment will be worth more than it was before.

Performance by Type of Fund

Obviously the kind of performance you will get depends on the type of fund.

In a *money market fund*, the question is simply one of *yield*—the income dividends you receive, as a percentage return on your investment.

Bond funds (both taxable and tax-exempt) are also usually bought primarily for dividend yield. But net asset value can go up or down, and this affects your total results. Also, bond funds may sometimes sell bonds at a profit and, as a result, pay capital gains distributions.

In *common stock funds*, income may also be important, but most shareholders are probably seeking long-term growth in the form of capital gains distributions and/or increases in net asset value. (See the discussion of different types of common stock funds in Chapter 7 above.)

Calculating Performance

Years ago, performance of common stock funds was usually calculated by adding only capital gains distributions and any rise in net asset value. The dividends paid were shown separately as "yield." This perhaps made sense for a shareholder who wanted or needed to spend the dividend income and wanted it clearly defined, but it was often difficult to compare different fund performances fairly with each other.

Now, most performance statistics are on what is called a "total return" basis, which takes all three elements into account, and shows how the value of a holder's investment would grow if all income dividends and capital gains distributions were reinvested in additional shares.

An example: Let's say that a fund starts a year with net asset value at $10.00 per share and ends with net asset value at $11.00. During the year it pays out $.40 per share in income dividends and $.70 per share in capital gains. Leaving aside certain minor adjustments, the quoted figures would be:

Yield (Dividend Income):

$$\frac{\$\ 0.40}{\$10.00} = 4.0\%$$

Performance—Old Definition:

$$\frac{(\$11.00 - \$10.00) + \$0.70}{\$10.00} = +17.0\%$$

Performance—Total Return (New Definition):

$$\frac{(\$11.00 - \$10.00) + \$0.70 + \$0.40}{\$10.00} = +21.0\%$$

In a bad year, of course, the net asset value of the fund could drop, and peformance could be negative rather than positive.

Performance of a common stock fund over short or long periods may be compared with other funds or with the "market averages." For example, a growth fund may be compared with an average of many growth funds. The funds are often compared with two or three well-known stock market averages that are found daily in your newspaper's financial section. One well-known stock market average is the Standard & Poor's 500 Stock Index, an index made up of 500 leading stocks. The Dow Jones Industrial Average is probably the most famous of all averages; however, as it is based on only 30 very prominent stocks, it is less of a reflection of the total market picture than the S&P

"500." The New York Stock Exchange Composite Index includes all 1500-or-so stocks listed on the New York Stock Exchange and tends to move proportionately to the S&P "500."

As a typical example of how funds use these performance comparisons, here is a slightly modified version of a table published in the report of the Weingarten Equity Fund (a very successful growth fund) for June 30, 1986:

Period ended June 30, 1986	Weingarten Equity Fund	Dow Jones Industrials	Standard & Poor's 500
	% Change*	% Change*	% Change*
6 months	+ 37%	+ 25%	+ 21%
1 year	+ 47%	+ 48%	+ 36%
5 years	+ 174%	+ 150%	+ 142%
10 years	+ 924%	+ 224%	+ 293%
15 years	+ 924%	+ 349%	+ 392%

*The Fund results assume the reinvestment of all capital gains and ordinary distribution income as of their record dates. The performance of the Fund is compared with that of the Dow Jones Industrial Average and the Standard & Poor's 500 Index, which are unmanaged and widely regarded as representative measurements of the stock market as a whole. Changes in the two indices assume reinvestment of all dividends based on data supplied by Lipper Analytical Services. The performance of the Fund should be considered in the light of its investment policy and objectives, the characteristics of the portfolio securities and the periods selected.

11 · SOURCES OF INFORMATION

Even if you intend to buy funds through a broker or sales-person, it is a good idea to familiarize yourself with some of the reliable sources of mutual fund information. If you are ready to do your own homework, you may find the prospect interesting and even exciting. And some of the sources that report on mutual fund performance and other statistics will also help you out with recommendations. They can't advise you as to what type of fund is right for you, but within the different groups they will help you in selecting better-quality funds.

Some publications show mutual fund performance for periods as short as the latest month or latest three months. This may be interesting, but you need a publication that shows how funds have done over longer periods—at least five years, preferably ten. You also need a source that classifies funds by type—that is, by investment objective—which is true of most of the sources listed below.

We have listed a few of the better publications, dividing them into those that provide performance statistics only and those that provide statistics plus recommendations. Some of these publications are too expensive to be practical for the average individual but may be carried by your local library—ask your librarian what's available. Or you may be able to consult them at a mutual fund office or investment firm.

Performance Statistics Only

Lipper Mutual Fund Performance Analysis (Lipper Analytical Securities Corp., 74 Trinity Place, New York, N.Y. 10006): This is the industry's leading source of performance statistics, and is widely quoted in other publications. Very expensive, and subscribed to primarily by professionals, but you may be able to find it at a library or elsewhere (see above). Issued weekly; special quarterly issues show performance over longer periods (usually five and ten years).

Computer Directions Advisors: Another detailed service primarily for professionals.

Performance Statistics and Other Data

Wiesenberger Investment Companies Service (Warren, Gorham & Lamont Inc., 1633 Broadway, New York, N.Y. 10019): The *Wiesenberger Investment Companies* annual yearbook is the bible of the fund industry, with extensive descriptions of funds, many chapters of information about the industry, all sorts of other data, and plentiful performance statistics. It is found in many libraries. There are also quarterly performance supplements.

Barron's: This national financial weekly (generally available on newsstands and at libraries) publishes special mutual fund surveys quarterly (in mid-February, May, August and November) featuring articles and some performance statistics.

Statistics and Recommendations

United Mutual Fund Selector (210 Newbury Street, Boston, MA 02116): Annual subscription $110. This excellent semimonthly newsletter features articles, performance statistics, and a recommended "Supervised List" of about 30 common stock funds classified by objective.

The No-Load Fund Investor (P.O. Box 283, Hastings-on-Hudson, N.Y. 10706): The annual *Handbook for No-Load Fund Investors* is $38; the *Handbook* plus monthly supplements is $100. Not quite as complete as Wiesenberger, but exceptionally useful and an excellent value. The statistics classify funds by objective, are clear and easy to read, and include recommendations.

Growth Fund Guide (Box 6600, Rapid City, SD 57709): Annual subscription $85. An excellent monthly publication covering selected no-load funds. Emphasizes the more aggressive growth funds, but lists a few middle-of-the-road funds as well. Recommendations classified by objective.

Money Magazine (generally available): *Money* publishes frequent mutual fund articles and extensive quarterly statistics on performance. It has become one of the most easily accessible sources of fund information.

Forbes Magazine (generally available): Every year in August or September, *Forbes* publishes a mutual fund survey featuring ten-year performance records of all funds, a few other statistics, and a brief "honor roll" of outstanding funds. Instead of the usual classifications, *Forbes* gives its own rankings of how funds have performed relatively in "up" and "down" markets.

In Sum

The recommendations of these sources are reasonably intelligent and fair, but don't hesitate to apply your own judgment to what you read. Look for funds that appear to fit your own particular objectives and preferences. Remember that even the best past record doesn't guarantee what a fund will achieve in the future.

Above all, don't pick a fund simply because it is near the top of the performance ratings for the latest year. A fund can do well over short periods for the wrong reasons—sometimes because management took more risks than really are prudent. But if a fund has done exceptionally well over a ten-year period, and still seems to be doing well, management apparently knows what it is doing.

Understanding the Statistics

A few warnings regarding performance statistics are in order:

1. Most of the statistics are presented in terms of percentage increases (+) or decreases (−). Sometimes the decreases may be shown by parentheses (25 percent) instead of a minus sign. Make sure you know how to read

these. Here is how a $10,000 investment would end up with various percentage changes:

−75% or (75%)	$ 2,500
−50% or (50%)	5,000
−25% or (25%)	7,500
0%	10,000
+25%	12,500
+50%	15,000
+100%	20,000
+150%	25,000
+200%	30,000
+300%	40,000
+400%	50,000

2. Remember that if the percentage figures are on a "total return" basis, any dividend yield is included. The statistics may also show yield separately, as a matter of interest; buy don't add this in to the total again.

3. If the statistics compare fund performance with stock market averages such as the Dow Jones Industrial Average or the Standard & Poor's 500 Stock Index, be careful. Fund performance will probably include income dividends ("yield"); but the market averages do *not* include income dividends, unless the publication makes a special adjustment. It's not hard for a fund to outshine the market averages if the fund is credited with 4 percent or 6 percent annually in income dividends and the averages are not. Read the footnotes carefully.

Contacting the Funds

When you have picked a few funds that look suitable, the next step is to send for their literature. Some of the publications named above do not include fund addresses or phone numbers. But you can get lists of funds by type, including addresses, from the Investment Company Institute, 1600 M Street, N.W., Washington, D.C. 20036 (202-293-7700), the trade association of the mutual fund industry. Ask them also for their general information booklets on funds. Lists covering no-load funds only are available from the No-Load Mutual Fund Association, 11 Penn Plaza, Suite 2204, New York, N.Y. 10001 (212-563-4540). You'll note that most of the major funds have toll-free "800" phone numbers that make it simple to request their literature.

12 · HOW TO READ A PROSPECTUS AND FINANCIAL REPORT

When you request information, a fund will typically send you a prospectus (a legal document that is the basic description of the fund and its policies) and its latest annual and quarterly reports to shareholders, as well as some miscellaneous sales literature.

Reading the Shareholder Reports

Most funds send reports to shareholders on a quarterly basis. These usually include a letter that reports on the fund's performance and current investment policies, and a list of the fund's investments ("portfolio"). The annual and semiannual reports include full financial statements showing the income and performance of the fund. (The financial statements may or may not be repeated in the prospectus.)

Read the letter to shareholders. What do the portfolio managers have to say about the current economic situation? How do they plan to act in the future? Does their investment outlook make sense to you? Are their goals the same as yours? Do they give a clear picture of what the fund has done over the last 3, 6, or 12 months?

Look at the portfolio list. See what types of securities the fund owns. Are you comfortable with them? Are the holdings varied in a way that makes sense to you? A stock fund may list its holdings by specific industry, or it may use such broad headings as "cyclical stocks," "consumer industries," etc.

Reading the Prospectus

Prospectuses are something of a puzzle. A fund can't legally sell shares to you until you have first received its prospectus. But many prospectuses are written in legal-type language that doesn't tell you as much as it should about the fund and its policies. Nevertheless, read the prospectus. If you still have questions, phone the fund office for the Statement of Additional Information that every fund must have available.

Nothing in the prospectus is more important than the statement of the fund's investment objective and policies. Read it carefully. Despite the occasional fuzziness and legal language, you should be able to get some idea of whether the fund's policies match what you are looking for, and whether you can feel comfortable with its approach.

Diversified and Non-diversified

You will notice that most funds are described in their prospectus as "diversified." A few are listed as "non-diversified." These are legal definitions. They sound important but in reality the difference is not great.

A "diversified" fund must keep 75 percent of its total portfolio diversified so that no single investment in that segment can make up more than 5 percent of the fund's total assets. (In the remaining 25 percent of the portfolio, management is free to concentrate in one or more larger positions if so desired.) A "non-diversified" company is only required to diversify 50 percent of its total portfolio and can concentrate investments within the remaining 50 percent.

Management

The prospectus will tell you about the management firm (the "investment adviser") and its affiliations. Usually it will list the directors and officers; if not, they can be found in the Statement of Additional Information. Most funds are required to have a certain number of directors who are *not* affiliated with the management firm; the law gives these "independent directors" many responsibilities intended to ensure fair treatment of the fund by the manager.

Management Fees

The fee paid to the fund's manager—termed the "investment advisory fee," or "management fee"—is generally the fund's largest single expense. The way the fee is calculated is stated in the prospectus. Most fees are calculated as a percentage of assets, and the fees usually work out to between 0.4 percent and 1.0 percent annually of the net assets.

If a fund's performance is well above average, don't be afraid of a higher-than-average fee; it's simply the manager's reward for having done a good job.

Fund Expenses

Let us turn back for a moment to the financial statements in the fund's shareholder reports. Near the bottom of the "Selected Per Share Data and Ratios" you will find a line showing the "Ratio of [annual] expenses to average net assets," commonly known as the fund's *expense ratio*. The expense ratio generally ranges from 0.5 percent to 1.5 percent—occasionally higher. If a fund receives dividends and interest on its portfolio that amount to 8.0 percent of average assets for a given year, and if the expense ratio for the year is 1.0 percent, then there will be 7.0 percent left to distribute to shareholders as income dividends.

How important is the expense ratio? If you buy a fund strictly for dividend yield, a high expense ratio is a disadvantage. But in a good growth fund, the expense ratio is a minor factor relative to total performance. If a fund has achieved a good past record in the face of a high expense ratio, there is no reason why it shouldn't continue to do so in the future. A high expense ratio doesn't usually mean poor management; more often it reflects a fund that is small in size, or a management fee that is a higher percentage than average.

Other Information

The prospectus will give you all sorts of additional information. It will tell you about the various shareholder conveniences described in Chapter 5. (Make sure the fund has the ones you want.) It will tell you when the fund pays dividends. It will tell you when the fund's fiscal (accounting) year ends, and when reports to shareholders are issued. (Annual reports must be mailed within 60 days after the close of the fiscal year; new prospectuses must be ready within 120 days.) It will tell you what organization (sometimes a bank, sometimes not) acts as the fund's shareholder servicing agent or transfer agent, and what bank (in this case it *must* be a bank) acts as custodian of the fund's cash and securities.

In either the annual report or the prospectus, or sometimes in both, you will find a certain amount of data on performance. By law there must be a ten-year table of "selected per share data and ratios," showing for each year the change in the fund's net asset value per share and the income dividends and capital gains distributions paid. You can calculate "total return" performance from these figures, but the table is not really convenient to use. Somewhere in the literature most funds include a more useful item, a chart showing an "illustration of an assumed investment of $10,000"—a chart showing how $10,000 invested in the fund would have grown over the last 10, 15, or 20 years, or for the whole life of the fund. The chart is usually clear enough, but the time period covered may be one that makes the figures hard to compare with those published by other funds. For comparisons of performance, you'll probably find that the figures compiled in the reference sources mentioned in Chapter 11 are easier and more practical to use than those published by the funds themselves.

Now we'll look at those sections of the prospectus that tell you how to go about purchasing and redeeming shares.

Ordering Shares

In a *load* fund, the prospectus will tell you how the load is calculated, and your broker or salesperson will explain the purchasing procedures. Most *no-load* and *low-load* funds enclose an order form with their prospectus and ask you to return the order form with a check. A smaller number will take your order by phone and send you a bill. (You must pay within five business days.) Some funds that require a written application to start will take subsequent orders by phone once the account is opened.

There are a few details about ordering shares that may not be made clear on the order form. If you are opening a joint account, note that joint accounts in the securities industry do *not* operate on the same "either/ or" basis as the usual joint account with a bank, where either owner acting alone can deposit or withdraw freely. Instead, the signatures of *both* owners are required on all important matters, including the redemption of shares. If you are purchasing shares for a minor, the usual procedure is to use the custodian arrangement permitted under the Uniform Gifts to Minors Acts in effect in all states. The correct form of registration is "Nancy Jones (one adult only) as custodian for David Jones (one minor only) under the Uniform Gifts to Minors Act of (state of residence of the minor)." The Social Security number given for the account should be that of the minor.

One piece of information that you will *not* find in the prospectus is a list of the states in which the fund's shares are registered for sale. If a fund is not registered for sale in the state in which you are a resident, you cannot buy shares in that fund. Even though the funds go through a careful registration process with the SEC every year, most of the states require separate registrations before the fund can be sold in that particular state. Most of the major funds are available for sale in all 50 states and the District of Columbia, but the cost and trouble of state registrations discourages some smaller funds from registering widely. For a load fund, your broker should know where the fund is registered; in the case of a no-load fund, phone the fund office or consult the Wiesenberger handbook.

Minimums

The prospectus will clearly state minimum purchase requirements. A typical stock fund may require $250 or $500 to open an account and a minimum of $100 on subsequent purchases. But the minimums vary widely. Money market funds and bond funds usually require larger amounts to start. Some funds reserve the right to redeem accounts that fall below the initial minimum, in order to save the fund the expense of maintaining a large number of small accounts.

Fractional Shares

Almost all mutual funds have accounting systems that can credit shareholders with fractional shares to three decimal places. For example, if you send a check for $1,000 to a no-load fund, and the fund is priced at $18.50 per share on the day your order is received, you will be credited with 54.054 shares. The fractional shares make it simple to buy or redeem shares in any desired dollar amount, with no odd pennies or dollars left over. If you insist on receiving stock certificates for your shares, you will find that the shareholder servicing agent won't issue certificates for fractional shares, and the fractions will have to be left on deposit. Most mutual fund shareholders have learned that it's far easier to leave all shares on deposit, and that stock certificates are an antiquated nuisance—particularly when you want to redeem the shares and the certificates have to be submitted. (See Chapter 18.)

Redemption Procedures

When you read a fund's prospectus, make sure that you understand the redemption procedures. (See Chapter 18.) And after you become a fund shareholder, when the fund mails you a new prospectus annually (as most funds do), see if the redemption section lists any new procedures. At some point you will probably want to redeem (sell) at least part of your shares, and when that time comes you don't want any surprises.

13 · HOW TO READ THE NEWSPAPER QUOTATIONS

One major advantage of a mutual fund is the ease with which you can follow the performance of a fund and the daily value of your investment. Every day, mutual fund prices are listed in the financial section of many newspapers, including the nationally available *Wall Street Journal.* Your fund may be listed in its alphabetical place, or if it is part of a major fund group, under the group heading (Dreyfus, Fidelity, Oppenheimer, Vanguard, etc.). Here is an excerpt from the *Wall Street Journal* listing showing prices of August 12, 1987:

	NAV	Offer Price	NAV Chg.
Mutl Beac	24.68	N.L.	+ .04
Mutl BnFd	16.37	17.89	+ .03
Mutual of Omaha Funds			
Amer	10.03	N.L.	...
Growth	9.05	9.84	− .04
Incom	9.58	10.41	− .01
Tax Free	11.06	12.02	+ .02
Mutl Fd	24.81	N.L.	+ .04
Mut Ql Shars	74.39	N.L.	+ .06
NtlAvia Tc	13.89	14.58	− .01
Natl Ind	15.56	N.L.	...

The fund names, obviously, are drastically abbreviated, but you will learn to recognize the funds you are interested in. The example shows a fund group (the Mutual of Omaha funds) and several individual funds that are not part of a large group.

"NAV" is the net asset value per share for each fund, calculated at the close of business on the given date. (See Chapter 9.) It is also the price that the fund paid for shares redeemed on that day (except in the cases where a redemption fee is charged). The "Offer Price" (offering price) column shows the price paid by investors who bought shares on that day—the net asset value plus the commission or "load." The abbreviation "N.L." means that the fund is *no-load* and that the price was the same for purchases as for redemptions—net asset value, with no commission added.

The right-hand column shows the change in net asset value compared with the previous day. Stock market prices averaged moderately lower on August 12, 1987 than on the previous day; some of the funds showed modest gains in net asset value, while others showed declines. Mutual of Omaha America Fund and National Industries Fund each showed no change on the day.

Some listings may show "bid" and "asked" instead of "NAV" and "Offering Price." These are old trading terms; the logic is that the fund will "bid" a certain price to buy your shares from you when you redeem, and will "ask" a certain price (the same price, in the case of a no-load fund) when you want to purchase shares from it.

When a fund price drops sharply because the shares have gone "ex-dividend" (see Chapter 16) that day, and the price has been marked down by the amount of the dividend, the price should be footnoted to explain this—the price in the "NAV" column might look like "x 7.66." But often the footnote is omitted. If you notice a sharp unexplained drop in the price of your fund, don't hesitate to phone the fund and ask about it. It may help to consult the prospectus to find out when dividends are usually paid.

14 · ONE FUND OR MANY?

We have frequently talked about "choosing the right fund for you." Perhaps we have made it sound as though one particular fund could be expected to meet all your investment needs. Of course, this isn't so.

If you have only $500 or $1,000 to invest, then on a practical basis you are better off beginning with one fund that meets your primary needs. But as your investment money grows, you can take into consideration more than one objective. You may want to have some money in a money market fund, to meet current needs and perhaps to take advantage of higher-than-normal interest rates. You may buy shares in a common stock fund for the primary objective of long-term growth. And if you are in a high tax bracket, you may also put some money in a municipal bond fund to generate tax-free income.

In addition to meeting your different objectives, this approach reduces risk by giving you even more diversification than you would have with a single fund. During a downward turn in the stock market, when your common stock fund is doing poorly, you may get particularly high income from your money fund and tax-exempt bond fund. Or the situation may be reversed. If you want the long-term growth that can come from common stocks, but find yourself worrying excessively over stock market price fluctuations, you may be particularly relieved to know that a certain percentage of your money is working in different directions.

But even if you are completely comfortable with all your money invested in common stocks, you find the price fluctuations manageable, and you don't want to sacrifice any of your growth potential, it may make sense to spread your money over a few funds rather than one. Different types of stocks perform differently at various times, and predictions are often difficult. One way to protect yourself is to divide your money among a few common stock funds with varying orientations. At the simplest level, you might own one aggressive growth fund and one growth-income fund. You can easily expand the selection as you go along to include funds that you find desirable. If you own a fund that concentrates on smaller growth companies, you may wish to add one that focuses on larger growth companies. And so on.

You might also want to put smaller slices of your money into more specialized funds. If you are worried about inflation, you might want some of your money in a gold fund, and some in a fund specializing in energy stocks. The possibilities are endless.

Even when choosing among funds of exactly the same type, diversification is usually the best policy. Which aggressive growth fund is the very best choice for the next ten years? While it's easy to see which fund in any group was the best choice for the *last* ten years, there's no way to be certain of the future. Rather than trying to decide which particular fund has the best prospects, it may be more reasonable to acknowledge the uncertainties of the situation and make up a package of a few funds that look promising. If one turns out disappointing, perhaps the others will more than make up for it.

15 · WHEN DO I BEGIN?

Should you try to adjust your mutual fund purchases to take advantage of market fluctuations?

Common stock prices tend to move in broad cycles. Sometimes the cycles seem to average about four years in length, but you can't be sure how any particular cycle will behave. Obviously, if you could pick one point at which to invest in common stock funds, it would be better in theory to invest at a point in the cycle when prices are low rather than when prices are high.

Bond prices also fluctuate. During much of the period from 1950 to 1982, interest rates were rising and, in reflection of this, bond prices suffered a long, painful decline. From mid-1982 to 1986, the trend went in the opposite direction, and bond prices showed major gains.

Unfortunately, predicting market movements is difficult even for the most expert professional, and an amateur can hardly hope to do better. However, an advantage of a mutual fund is that, in a diversified portfolio, movements in some portfolio securities are likely to offset movements in others, and fluctuations in the value of the fund's shares are likely to be less extreme than fluctuations in the prices of individual securities. Also, a good manager may be successful in insulating a fund to some extent from declines in the general market. But even the best-managed fund is likely to move to some extent with the general market trend.

Many amateur investors react to market fluctuations in exactly the wrong way. They tend to buy securities toward the end of a long market rise, when everyone has gotten overenthusiastic; and they panic and sell near the end of a decline, just when the market is about to turn up. There are a few useful things you can do to guard against making this kind of mistake:

1. Recognize that this is an uncertain area, and distrust the person who tells you that the market is "bound to go up" or "bound to go down."

2. Recognize that markets are subject to fads, and that fads are dangerous. Try to avoid crowd psychology. When stock prices are rising and the XYZ fund has gone up 50 percent or 100 percent, and everyone tells you that this is the time to buy, be careful: prices may be near a peak.

3. Consider spacing out your purchases on a regular schedule. For the average investor, this is probably the best approach of all. If you can invest, say, $500 every three months, and keep this up over a period of years, you will do some buying when prices are high and some when prices are low, and you will end up with a reasonable cost average over the long term without running the danger of having to make market predictions. This approach is often termed "dollar-cost averaging." For example, if you have never bought a mutual fund and if, at the end of reading this book, you have decided to take $10,000 out of a savings account to buy a good common stock fund—don't do your buying all at once. Space it out in installments over a year or two. In that way, if it happens to be a period when prices are declining, you won't have the depressing experience of having completed all your buying just before the market dips.

This kind of regular purchase program does more than simply guarantee you a reasonable average cost. If you develop the habit of making regular purchases and stick to it over the years, you will have achieved the kind of long-run savings program that almost everyone intends to follow but that few people actually achieve. As you build up a savings cushion, you are likely to find that market fluctuations become less and less a source of worry, and that your money is managing to compound and grow beyond your expectations.

16 · TIMING AND DIVIDENDS

Although we have already discussed dividends (Chapter 10), we haven't mentioned a small point about the relation of dividends to the timing of your mutual fund purchases.

When a fund's board of directors declares a dividend and sets a payment date, it also sets the "ex-dividend" date. ("Ex-dividend" means "without dividend.") New shares purchased on this date (or after) are no longer entitled to receive the dividend. But this really doesn't matter, since, as an offset, the *price per share is automatically marked down exactly by the amount of the dividend.*

So don't ever let anyone tell you to buy shares of a mutual fund before a certain date, in order to "get the dividend." You get the dividend, sure enough, but you pay a higher price because of it.

It makes more sense to buy *after* the ex-dividend date. Here's why: Putting aside market variations, the price you pay on the ex-dividend date or later, as we said above, is marked down precisely to compensate you for not getting the dividend. *But since you don't receive the dividend, you don't have to pay income tax on it.* If you buy before the ex-date, the dividend you get offsets the higher price you pay, but you are actually worse off by the amount of the tax you will have to pay on the dividend.

So when a fund is about to pay a dividend or capital gains distribution—especially a big one—wait to buy until after the ex-dividend date.

As pointed out in Chapter 13, the newspaper listings often fail to show the "ex-dividend" price changes correctly. When a fund's price drops sharply because the shares have gone "ex-dividend" that day, there should be a footnote of explanation. But often the footnote is omitted. (See Chapter 13 for more on this point.)

17 · TO SELL OR NOT TO SELL

Deciding when to sell mutual fund shares can be just as puzzling as deciding when to buy. Again, an amateur should be wary of believing anyone who claims to know just what the stock market or bond market is about to do. But again, there are some guidelines that will help you make your selling decisions intelligently.

There are three basic situations in which you are likely to consider selling (redeeming) fund shares:

Reason for Redeeming #1—To Raise Cash

You need money—perhaps unexpectedly, perhaps as part of a long-range plan. If it is a planned event—if you are buying a house, or taking out money for a child's college tuition—don't wait until the last minute, since you might be forced to redeem just at a time when the market is depressed. Consider redeeming 6 to 18 months before you actually need the money, and let the cash sit safely in a money market fund or bank market-rate account until you are ready to use it.

Reason for Redeeming #2—To Switch

What if you have doubts about a particular fund you own? An investment in a good fund doesn't have to be watched as closely as an individual stock, but neither can you ignore it entirely. Every few months (or as frequently as you wish) you should review your holdings carefully and ask yourself the following questions:

- Has there been any change in my investment situation or objective?
- Am I satisfied with the fund(s) I own?
- If I were starting fresh today, would I pick the same fund(s) that I actually now own?

The last question is critical. If there are reasons to prefer a fund you don't own over one you do, think carefully. If the reasons are serious and not trivial, don't hesitate to switch. Even the best fund sometimes turns mediocre. Sometimes a good manager simply doesn't cope well with a new and different stage in the economy. No matter how well a fund has served you, *don't become emotionally attached to it.* On the other hand, don't switch out of a good fund just because it has shown poor performance for a very short period.

If your fund shares are now worth more than they originally cost you, you may have a capital gains tax to pay if you sell. (See Chapter 19.) But it is probably a mistake to let this stand in your way. It is usually worth paying the tax in order to follow your best judgment and have your money invested in the funds that appear to suit you best right now.

Reason for Redeeming #3—Market Conditions

Some investors like to sell their mutual fund shares when they feel that the stock market (or the bond market, as the case may be) is in danger of a major decline, in the hope of avoiding the decline and perhaps buying back their shares at a lower price.

Logically at least, this makes sense. The stock market does move in cycles, and if you can sell at the top and buy at the bottom you will certainly be well off. The trouble is that the timing of these cycles is quite uncertain, and while the major turning points are easy to see in retrospect a year or two later, they can be very hard to recognize when they are taking place. Many investors, unfortunately, sell their shares in the panic atmosphere that exists when the stock market is near a low point, which is just the time when it would be best to buy. They then either (1) fail to buy the shares back or (2) buy them at just the wrong time—when everyone has become enthusiastic and stock prices are at or near a high point.

So the average investor is probably better off simply

buying and holding mutual fund shares for the long pull—
and spacing out fund purchases as discussed in Chapter 15
so that all buying is not concentrated near a market top.

However, if you decide that you do want to try to
"catch" these cycles, here are a few thoughts to keep in
mind.

Stock Market Fluctuations

While stock market cycles are usually hard to judge at
the time they are taking place, there are some indicators that professional investors use to try to understand
and forecast price movements. Some of these indicators
depend on the state of the economy; some are based on the
patterns of the stock market itself. The stock market often
anticipates changes in the economy. Major market upturns
have often begun near the end of a recession, when everyone is full of doom and gloom. Major downturns have
often begun near the end of a period of prosperity and
rising interest rates. If you want to "catch the cycle" successfully, you need to have the courage to buy when most
people are gloomy and sell when most people are enthusiastic.

Long-Term Headaches in the Bond Market

In Chapter 7, we explained why we think that the average
investor may be better off avoiding long-term bonds and
long-term bond funds. Movements in interest rates and
bond prices have been even more difficult to predict than
movements in the stock market. But while the long-term
trend in stock prices has been *upward*—rewarding the
common stock investor who rode out the fluctuations—
the long-term trend in bond prices for most of the postwar
period has been *downward*—reflecting the long, grinding
climb in interest rates. So rather than advising you when to
sell long-term bonds, we will repeat our earlier advice:
Invest in them only with great caution.

Tax-Exempts: Whether to Buy and Hold

In Chapter 7 we also explained that for someone in a high tax bracket, the high net yield after taxes available from a tax-exempt fund might justify taking the risk of a price decline. If you think you can predict when such a decline in bond prices is coming, of course it makes sense to sell. But if tax-exempt income is what you need, it's equally reasonable simply to pick a fund that has had an outstanding record over several years, hope that the yield will be high enough to compensate for any price declines, and hope that the fund managers will be smart enough to hold such declines to a minimum.

18 · HOW TO REDEEM YOUR SHARES

Having discussed the reasons why you might wish to sell your mutual fund shares, we would like to discuss briefly the procedures you will need to follow when you decide to redeem.

Remember that mutual fund shares are not traded on an open market like most common stocks. Rather, the fund itself stands ready to redeem (buy back) your shares on any business day when you wish to sell. For most funds, the redemption price is the net asset value per share (see Chapter 9) calculated on the day the fund receives your order; but some funds, as mentioned earlier, impose a redemption fee which is deducted from your proceeds.

Your redemption order will only be valid if you follow the fund's stated procedures. Read this part of your fund's prospectus carefully. Most stock and bond funds—or their shareholder servicing agents—require a letter of instructions with signature(s) guaranteed, for a redemption. If there are joint owners, all owners must sign the letter, and all signatures must be guaranteed. A guarantee protects against an unauthorized person redeeming your shares. You must secure this guarantee from your commercial bank or from a brokerage firm that is a member of a national securities exchange. Note that most funds do *not* accept guarantees by savings banks or savings and loan associations. If you hold certificates for shares being redeemed, the certificates must also be submitted, with guaranteed signatures on the reverse or on an accompanying "stock power" form. (This, again, is a reason to leave your shares on deposit with the agent and not to bother holding certificates.)

Some funds waive the signature guarantee requirement on smaller redemptions, especially if the stock is in the name of a single owner. When there are joint owners, the fund usually wants to be sure that one owner is not redeeming without the knowledge of the other. In the case of trusts, estates, corporations or other entities, the fund will often require additional documents for redemption—check with the fund or servicing agent in advance.

Under the law, the fund must mail a check to you within seven days after the redemption date. However, this mailing may be delayed if you bought your shares just before redeeming them and your purchase check hasn't yet cleared.

Simplified Redemptions

Most money market funds make redemptions much easier. Usually you can write a check on your money fund account. (The fund pays the check by redeeming a certain number of your shares.) Or you can phone the fund and request that shares be redeemed and a check mailed to you or that the money be wired directly to your bank account.

With the money funds having shown the way, the trend in other funds is also toward simpler redemption procedures. Many bond and stock funds now let shareholders request the telephone redemption privilege, and some bond funds will also let you write checks on your account. (To cover the check, shares are redeemed at whatever the current price happens to be.)

If your fund is part of a "family of funds," you can usually arrange for *switches* by telephone. If the group has a money market fund, you can switch into it by telephone and then take advantage of the more convenient redemption procedures that most money market funds provide.

The Tax Impact

Remember that when you redeem shares, you have probably realized a capital gain or loss for tax purposes, and Uncle Sam is definitely looking over your shoulder. We'll discuss income taxes in Chapter 19.

19 · TAXES AND RECORD-KEEPING

The tax law gives mutual funds and their shareholders a special break. Although most funds are corporations, they escape usual corporate income taxes by *passing through* income and capital gains to their shareholders. The shareholder pays the tax, but the fund doesn't.

You owe income taxes on the income dividends and capital gains distributions you receive from a fund. If you sell your fund shares at a profit, you owe a tax on the capital gain.

Dividends and Distributions

If your total income dividends and capital gains distributions from a fund in a given calendar year exceed $10, the fund sends you a Form 1099-DIV* the following January summarizing these distributions and listing the amounts you need to report on your income tax return. The fund sends the original of this form to the IRS, so that the agency has an easy way of spotting delinquent or careless taxpayers.

The income dividends paid by a mutual fund are reported on your tax return like dividends from any other corporation. If the fund has paid out any short-term capital gains, this amount will probably be included in the dividend amount on your Form 1099-DIV. Long-term capital gains distributions are shown separately.

However, the distinctions between long-term capital gains, short-term capital gains and dividend income are far less important than they used to be. The Tax Reform Act of 1986, in a sweeping change, completely eliminated the traditional favorable treatment of long-term capital gains.

---

*In this chapter we describe tax forms by their 1986-87 names and numbers. The IRS will undoubtedly make changes as time goes by.

A slight tax break for long-term gains was retained for 1987, but beginning in 1988, long-term capital gains are taxed at the same rates as other types of income. (For more information on the Tax Reform Act of 1986, see the No Nonsense Financial Guide, *The New Tax Law and What It Means to You.*)

Many people think that some preferential treatment of long-term gains will be revived in the future. Meanwhile, the tax law (and probably the tax forms) will continue to distinguish long-term gains from other income, even if the tax rates are the same.

More Fallout from the Tax Reform Act

Mutual fund shareholders were also affected by some of the other steps taken in the 1986 tax law to eliminate "special breaks." One of the breaks that was done away with was the dividend exclusion. The old tax law permitted taxpayers to *exclude* the first $100 of dividends from income subject to tax ($200 on a joint return). The 1986 law eliminated this exclusion.

In a more serious change, the 1986 law introduced a complicated treatment of mutual fund expenses that could cause mutual fund shareholders to pay taxes on higher amounts than the dividends they actually receive from a fund. This provision of the law is so cumbersome that there is hope that Congress may take action to eliminate it.

Capital Gain or Loss on Redemptions

When you redeem shares in any type of fund other than a money market fund, you usually have a capital gain or loss for tax purposes, depending on whether the redemption price is more or less than your original cost. The profit or loss must be reported on your tax return (on Schedule D of Form 1040).

When you switch from one fund to another within a group of funds, the redemption of shares from the first fund counts as a sale for tax purposes, like any other redemption. And in an automatic withdrawal plan, any redemptions of shares done monthly or quarterly to provide you with withdrawal checks also are redemptions like any others for tax purposes.

Money market funds, of course, are the exception. As long as a money market fund follows a policy of keeping its share price constant (usually at $1.00 per share), there is no gain or loss when you liquidate shares.

If you have redeemed shares during the year, the fund sends the IRS a notice after the end of the year showing the dollar amounts redeemed, with a copy to you (Form 1099-B). The IRS doesn't know which of your transactions were profitable and which were not, but it will probably check your tax return to make sure that you reported either a capital gain or capital loss corresponding to each redemption.

A Few Points Worth Noting

You should be aware that none of the usual mutual fund performance statistics make any allowance or deduction for the taxes you have to pay along the way. Since every shareholder may be in a different tax bracket, there's no way to build the tax bite into the statistics. Obviously, if you have to take money out of your fund account to pay taxes, it will limit the buildup of your investment.

Also note that you are required to pay taxes on dividends and capital gains distributions, whether or not you reinvest these distributions in additional shares. From a tax standpoint, the reinvestment is treated no differently than if you received the cash and used this cash to buy more shares.

None of the above applies to retirement plan accounts such as IRAs (Individual Retirement Accounts) and self-employed retirement plans (Keogh plans), which will be dealt with briefly in the next chapter. The law exempts those accounts from current taxes, so that they earn and compound tax-free until the money is taken out.

Record-Keeping

Now for a brief note about record-keeping.

Mutual funds greatly simplify your record-keeping problems. But there are a few things that you should still do. When you receive the confirmation of a purchase, redemption or dividend, look at it to make sure you know what was done and that the confirmation is correct. After the end of the year, check your copy of the Form 1099-DIV that the fund sends to you to make sure it makes sense. Also, if you have redeemed shares during the year, check the Form 1099-B that the fund sends to you. Remember, as we said above, a redemption of any type is a sale of shares, which gives rise to a capital gain or loss for tax purposes.

Above all, *keep your records of share purchases*, including shares purchased through dividend reinvestment. Some day you are likely to sell your shares, and for tax purposes you will need to know what they originally cost. If your fund sends you a year-end statement showing all of your transactions for the calendar year, make that your prime item to file and keep.

20 · USING THE FUNDS FOR YOUR IRA AND KEOGH

In Chapter 5, we mentioned that most mutual funds offer simple arrangements for investing in an IRA (Individual Retirement Account) or self-employed retirement plan (Keogh plan).

The subject is worth returning to briefly. Prior to 1982, IRAs were only for persons who were not covered under any other retirement plan. Beginning in 1982, IRAs were opened to everyone who works for a living, whether covered by another retirement plan or not. The IRA became the first major tax break in history for the individual saver—in effect, a *tax shelter for everyone*. The law permitted anyone with *earned income* to deposit up to $2,000 a year (or up to the amount of earned income, whichever is less) into a tax-sheltered IRA and to take an income tax deduction for the amount set aside.

IRAs and the New Tax Law

The Tax Reform Act of 1986 preserved the basic structure of IRAs, but put restrictions on the tax deduction. Now, if you participate in any employer's retirement plan, you can still put up to $2,000 in an IRA, but you can only take the tax deduction if your income is below certain specified levels. On the other hand, if you do *not* participate in any employer's plan, you can still take the full tax deduction, whatever your income.

Most important, there's no change in the rule that the money in an IRA *earns and compounds tax-free* until withdrawn. Over a period of 15 or 20 years or more, this tax-free accumulation (technically, it's *tax-deferred*) can do more to build up your money than the original tax deduction. (For more information, see the No Nonsense Financial Guide, *Understanding IRAs*.)

Mutual funds can be an excellent investment for an

IRA or for a retirement plan of any type. For a younger person in particular, an IRA is a long-term investment that is ideal for common stocks and common stock funds. If you can select funds with good long-term growth rates, and let this growth compound, the long-term buildup of your money can be dramatic. For anyone who is eligible for an IRA, tax deduction or not, this is a possibility worth thinking about.

If you want to be more conservative, you can consider long-term bond funds as an IRA investment. Although we have recommended that long-term bonds be approached with caution, they can be an attractive investment for a retirement plan at times when interest rates are high and bond prices low.

Keogh Plan Opportunities

The same arguments apply to self-employed retirement plans, popularly known as "Keogh" plans. Here the contribution limits were raised sharply in 1984 and now range up to $30,000 annually or more, depending on an individual's tax bracket and the type of plan chosen. If you are a businessman or professional, working as a sole proprietor or in a partnership, and can afford to make sizable contributions to a Keogh plan, your buildup for the future in a growth investment can be staggering. Even if you are a person who simply has some self-employment income on the side, in addition to a regular job, a Keogh plan makes sense for whatever contributions you can afford.

Choices at Retirement

When you are ready to begin taking money out of an IRA or Keogh, a fund automatic withdrawal plan is a simple way to provide regular cash withdrawals while keeping the balance of your plan working for you in the type of fund you prefer. Or, if you receive a lump-sum distribution from an employer's retirement plan, you can take the same approach by putting the money in a "rollover" IRA and then taking periodic withdrawals. In any of these cases, you pay income tax each year only on the amount actually withdrawn, while the balance remaining in your retirement account continues to earn on a tax-deferred basis. (For more information, see the No Nonsense Financial Guide, *How to Plan and Invest for Your Retirement.*)

If, at retirement, you want to be sure of your dollars and take less risk of fluctuations, the money market funds provide an obvious answer, and you can easily arrange to switch part or all of your plan into the money market fund of your choice.

21 · GROWTH AND INCOME: THE BEST OF BOTH WORLDS

This is a bonus chapter. Its purpose is to leave you with an extra idea that may help you and that you may not easily learn elsewhere. It is especially important for readers who need some spendable income from their investments.

Refer back for a moment to Chapter 3. We talked about investing for growth and obtaining spendable income. These are usually talked about as requiring very different investment approaches. If you need spendable income, you will often be advised to keep at least part of your money in more conservative investments that sacrifice growth possibilities to obtain dependable interest or dividends.

But this approach carries penalties. Over the long run the best total results have been achieved by investors who invest (carefully) for *growth*. Over 10-year or 15-year periods, investors who have put money in the better common stock *growth* funds have done far better than investors in bonds, money market funds, or even more conservative stock funds. In the ten years 1977–86 the *average* growth fund achieved a total return that worked out to *over 15 percent annually*, compounded. Several of the best-performing growth funds averaged well over 20 percent annually. Is it worth giving up that potential and sticking to low-growth or no-growth investments because you need perhaps 8 percent or 10 percent spendable income?

Of course, there may be more involved than your need for income. You may be happy only with an investment that gives you a dependable return every year, and you may simply be too uncomfortable with the price fluctuations of a typical growth fund.

But if you can take a long-run approach and are willing to live with price fluctuations, there's another way out.

With a mutual fund you can go for growth and, in effect, *spend* part of the growth as you go along. Here's how:

Say you owned a "just average" growth fund during the years 1977–86. As stated above, this average fund would have shown a total return of above 15 percent annually—in fact, about 17 percent. Let's assume that this total included dividends of 2 percent annually, capital gains distributions averaging 5 percent annually, and growth in the price of the shares averaging 10 percent annually. Let's also assume that you needed a 10 percent *spendable* return.

To get your 10 percent spendable return, you would have sold an average of 3 percent of your shares every year, and the cash from these sales would have supplemented what you got from the income dividends and capital gains distributions. Nevertheless, because the price per share of your fund was growing at a rate of 10 percent annually, the total market value of your remaining shares would still have grown by 7 percent annually.

While a fund's income dividends are usually consistent from year to year, capital gains distributions are likely to vary widely, depending on what gains or losses the fund has taken in its portfolio transactions. In years when your fund's capital gains distributions were large, you would have sold fewer shares to raise cash; in years when the distributions were small or nonexistent, you would have sold more. Remember that the figures we have given are in terms of *averages*. On the *average*, you would have sold 3 percent of your shares per year; and on the *average*, the price of your fund would have gained 10 percent per year; but the year-to-year figures would have fluctuated quite widely.

We should point out that the decade 1977–86 was a very good period for the stock market—in many other periods your results would not have been that favorable. But by taking a long-run point of view, you can achieve excellent results with good common stock funds.

An easy way mechanically of taking money out of your fund on a regular basis is by setting up an automatic withdrawal plan. You instruct the fund regarding the amount of the check you want to receive monthly or quarterly, and the fund redeems just enough shares each time to provide the necessary cash. Many fund shareholders have used this arrangement with satisfaction. In many cases (depending on the market situation and the size of withdrawals) they have been able to withdraw the needed spendable money and still see some growth in the value of their remaining shares.

What are the drawbacks? First, this approach only works if you are investing for the long run. Growth funds have good years and bad years; you need to follow the approach long enough for the basic growth trend to work out. Second, you have to set yourself a reasonable schedule and stick to it. In a bad year, when the market is down and your fund may drop 10 percent or more in value, it may feel uncomfortable to reduce your holding an additional 6 percent to 10 percent by withdrawals; you need to have confidence that your program is reasonable, and that you will make up the "deficit" in the next good year, when your fund may be up 20 percent or 25 percent. Obviously, you need to take great care in your choice of fund. You need to apply the principles discussed in Chapter 10, watch the results carefully (Chapters 11 and 13), and don't be afraid to switch if your fund does badly for six months or a year relative to funds of the same type.

Note how perfectly mutual funds fit into this investment approach: (1) You have a very wide choice of growth funds offering different degrees of risk and managed by outstanding professionals. (2) You can invest money and take money out in relatively small amounts and with great flexibility. In some other types of investment—for example, real estate property—it may be hard to "spend" part of your growth in value without selling the whole investment or taking out an expensive loan. If you were to invest in common stocks directly, it would be relatively expensive to buy and sell in smaller amounts. (3) You can have the extra convenience of an automatic withdrawal plan.

For convenience in this type of operation, it is hard to

match a good mutual fund—or a few good mutual funds. (We are certainly not suggesting that you have to limit yourself to one.)

So if you need income but want growth as well—consider the message of this chapter, choose your funds carefully, and you may well be able to enjoy the best of both worlds.

GLOSSARY

Adviser See Investment Adviser.

Automatic Reinvestment A plan by which income dividends and/or capital gains distributions are automatically applied to buy additional shares of a mutual fund.

Balanced Fund See Chapter 7.

Bond A long-term debt security issued by a government or corporation promising repayment of a given amount by a given date, plus interest.

Bond Fund A mutual fund investing primarily in bonds.

Book Shares Shares of a fund owned by an investor and recorded on the books of a fund without a certificate being issued.

Broker-Dealer A term including several types of firms in the securities business who usually do business with the public.

Capital Wealth invested or available for investment.

Capital Gain The profit from sale of a security or other asset at a price above its cost.

Capital Gains Distribution A payment by a mutual fund to its shareholders derived from capital gains realized by the fund on sales of securities in its portfolio.

Certificate In a mutual fund, a document showing ownership of a certain number of shares.

Common Stock A security representing a share of ownership in a corporation.

Common Stock Fund   A mutual fund investing primarily in common stocks.

Custodian   The organization (usually a bank) that holds in safekeeping the securities and other assets of a mutual fund.

Dealer   See Broker-Dealer.

Distributor   The organization that distributes the mutual fund's shares to broker-dealers and/or the public.

Diversification   For a mutual fund, the practice of spreading investments over several different securities to reduce risk.

Dividend   A share of earnings paid to a shareholder by a mutual fund or other corporation.

Dividend Reinvestment   See Automatic Reinvestment.

Dollar Cost Averaging   Investing equal amounts of money at regular intervals. (See Chapter 15.)

Ex-Dividend, Ex-Dividend Date   See Chapter 16.

Expense Ratio   See Chapter 12.

Income Dividends   Payments to mutual fund shareholders derived from interest and dividends earned by the fund on its portfolio securities.

Index Fund   A mutual fund that holds a large number of stocks selected and weighted to match the performance of a stock market index or average.

Investment Adviser   The organization that a mutual fund pays for investment advice and, usually, general business management. The adviser is usually also the sponsor and promoter of the fund.

Investment Advisory Fee   The fee paid by the fund to the adviser. (See Chapter 12.)

Investment Company A company in which many investors pool their money for investment. Mutual funds are the most popular type.

Issued Shares In a mutual fund, shares for which certificates are issued.

Liquid Asset Fund A money market fund.

Liquid Investment An investment that can be converted easily into cash, without penalty.

Load The sales charge or commission charged on purchase of some mutual funds.

Management Fee See Investment Advisory Fee.

Money Market Fund A mutual fund that aims at maximum safety, liquidity, and (usually) a constant price for its shares. Its assets are invested to earn current market interest rates on the safest, short-term, highly liquid investments.

Municipal Bond A bond issued by a state or local government. The interest is usually exempt from federal income tax.

Mutual Fund See this whole book.

Net Asset Value, Net Asset Value Per Share See Chapter 9.

No-Load Fund A mutual fund that sells its shares at net asset value, without any commission.

Offering Price See Chapter 13.

Open-End Investment Company A mutual fund. Technically called "open-end" because the fund stands ready to sell new shares to investors or to buy back shares submitted for redemption.

Portfolio   The total list of securities owned by a mutual fund or by any investor.

Portfolio Manager   An individual who makes decisions regarding buying, selling, or holding securities for an investment organization.

Principal   The capital or main body of an investment, as distinguished from the income earned on it.

Prospectus   The official document describing a mutual fund and offering its shares for sale. See Chapter 12.

Redemption   The procedure by which a mutual fund buys back shares from shareholders on demand.

Redemption Price   See Chapters 9 and 18.

SEC   The U.S. Securities and Exchange Commission: The federal agency charged with regulating securities markets and the investment industry (including mutual funds).

Security   General term meaning stocks, bonds and other investment instruments.

Shareholder-Servicing Agent   The bank or other organization that maintains a fund's shareholder records and processes shareholder transactions.

Stock   A security representing an ownership interest in a corporation.

Transfer Agent   See Shareholder Servicing Agent.

Underwriter or Principal Underwriter   See Distributor.

Unissued Shares   In a mutual fund, this term refers to book shares. (See Book Shares.)

Withdrawal Plan   A plan by which a mutual fund shareholder receives regular periodic checks (usually monthly or quarterly) from his or her investment. The checks are derived from accumulated dividends or capital gains distributions and/or automatic redemptions of shares.

Yield   The return on an investment. In securities, the dividends or interest received, usually expressed as an annual percentage of either the current market value or the cost of the investment.

TABLE A
Selected Larger Common Stock Funds

Name	15 Years		5-Year Total % Gain (a)	Load/ No-Load	Telephone Number
	Total % Gain (a)	Annual Growth Rate			
AGGRESSIVE GROWTH FUNDS					
American Capital Comstock	855%	16.2%	131%	load	800-231-3638
American Capital Pace	829	16.0	143	load	800-231-3638
AMEV Growth Fund	739	15.2	146	load	800-872-2638
Charter Fund	745	15.3	91	load	800-231-0803
Janus Fund	751	15.3	128	no-load	800-525-3713
Putnam Voyager Fund	742	15.3	136	load	800-225-1581
SteinRoe Special Fund	655	14.4	169	no-load	800-621-0320
Tudor Fund	602	13.9	155	no-load	800-223-3332
Twentieth Century Growth Investors	1,523	20.4	92	no-load	800-345-2021
Weingarten Equity Fund	734	15.2	167	load	800-231-0803
GROWTH FUNDS					
Acorn Fund (b)	668	14.6	136	no-load	312-621-0630
AMCAP Fund	578	13.6	116	load	800-421-9900
Columbia Growth Fund	453	12.1	137	no-load	800-547-1037
Evergreen Fund	1,244	18.9	138	no-load	800-235-0064
Fidelity Magellan Fund	1,722	21.3	271	3% load	800-544-6666
International Investors (c)	1,553	20.6	68	load	800-221-2220
NEL Growth Fund	623	14.1	197	load	800-343-7104
New York Venture Fund	656	14.4	171	load	800-545-2098
Nicholas Fund	472	12.3	168	no-load	800-227-5987
Over-The-Counter Securities (b)	950	17.0	114	load	800-523-2578
Partners Fund	577	13.6	147	no-load	800-367-0770
Templeton Growth Fund (d)	1,335	19.4	133	load	800-237-0738
Twentieth Century Select Investors	1,483	20.2	175	no-load	800-345-2021
GROWTH AND INCOME FUNDS					
Affiliated Fund	577	13.6	161	load	800-223-4224
American Capital Harbor	498	12.7	146	load	800-231-3638
American Mutual Fund	656	14.4	165	load	800-421-9900
AMEV Capital Fund	522	13.0	166	load	800-872-2638
Dodge & Cox Stock Fund	448	12.0	168	no-load	415-981-1710
Guardian Mutual Fund	612	14.0	143	no-load	800-367-0770

TABLE A (*Continued*)

Name	15 Years Total % Gain (a)	Annual Growth Rate	5-Year Total % Gain (a)	Load/ No-Load	Telephone Number
GROWTH AND INCOME FUNDS					
Investment Co. of America	528	13.0	178	load	800-421-9900
Mutual Shares Corp.	1,294	19.2	164	no-load	800-457-0211
Pioneer II	1,149	18.3	129	load	800-225-6292
Sentinel Common Stock	555	13.3	181	load	800-233-4332
Washington Mutual Investors	634	14.2	199	load	800-421-9900
COMMON STOCK INCOME (EQUITY INCOME) FUNDS					
American National Income	628	14.2	119	load	800-231-4639
Decatur Fund—Decatur I Series	571	13.5	163	load	800-523-4640
Fidelity Equity-Income Fund (e)	869	16.3	181	2% load	800-544-6666
Fidelity Puritan Fund (e)	601	13.9	179	2% load	800-544-6666
Financial Industrial Income	656	14.4	166	no-load	800-525-8085
Franklin Income Series (e)	514	12.9	158	load	800-632-2180
Income Fund of America (e)	537	13.1	171	load	800-421-9900
National Total Return Fund	513	12.8	146	load	800-223-7757
Oppenheimer Equity Income	828	16.0	172	load	800-525-7048
SAFECO Income Fund (e)	598	13.8	173	no-load	800-426-6730

(a) Percent increase in value of an investment over the fifteen years 1972–1986 and the five years 1982–1986, assuming all income dividends and capital gains distributions reinvested. For the fifteen-year period, the average annual compounded growth rate also is shown. No deduction has been made for any commission (load) paid or for any income taxes payable on dividends and distributions. Common stock prices generally declined in 1973–74 and generally rose over the period 1975–1986; the total return figures shown above are a record of the past, and should not be taken as an indication of future results.

(b) Fund specializing in stocks of smaller growth companies.

(c) Fund specializing in gold-mining stocks.

(d) Substantial portion of fund's assets may be in foreign securities.

(e) Fund's portfolio may include a substantial proportion of bonds and/or preferred stocks.

Note: Total return statistics derived from data published in *Lipper—Mutual Fund Performance Analysis*, December 31, 1986, published by Lipper Analytical Services, Inc.

TABLE B
SELECTED LARGER TAXABLE BOND FUNDS

Name	Total Return (a)		Minimum Initial Investment	Telephone Number
	10 Yrs.	5 Yrs.		
NO-LOAD FUNDS				
Axe-Houghton Income Fund	194%	139%	$1,000	800-431-1030
Babson Bond Trust	152	118	500	800-821-5591
Fidelity High Income Fund (b)	—	163	2,500	800-544-6666
Fidelity Intermediate Bond Fund	197	111	1,000	800-544-6666
Keystone B-1 (c)	169	128	250	800-225-1587
Keystone B-2 (c)	194	119	250	800-225-1587
Northeast Investors Trust	187	160	500	800-225-6704
LOAD FUNDS				
Bond Fund of America	190	138	1,000	800-421-9900
Delchester Bond Fund	175	144	25	800-523-4640
IDS Bond Fund (d)	192	152	2,000	800-328-8300
IDS Selective Fund	183	156	2,000	800-328-8300
Kemper High Yield Fund (b)	—	163	1,000	800-621-1148
Lord Abbett U.S. Govt. Securities Fund	183	125	500	800-223-4224
Mass. Financial High Income Trust (b)	—	150	250	800-343-2829
Putnam Income Fund	168	136	500	800-225-1581

(a) Percent increase in value of an investment over the ten years 1977–1986 and the five years 1982–1986, assuming all income dividends and capital gains distributions reinvested. No deduction has been made for any commission (load) paid or for any income taxes payable on dividends and distributions. Bond prices generally declined over the period 1977–1981 and generally rose over the period 1982–1986; the total return figures shown above are a record of the past, and should not be taken as an indication of future results.

(b) "High-yield" fund which may invest a substantial portion of its assets in lower-rated bonds.

(c) Fee may be charged on redemptions.

(d) Low-load fund.

Note: Total return statistics derived from data published in *Lipper—Fixed Income Fund Performance Analysis*, December 31, 1986, and *Lipper—Mutual Fund Performance Analysis*, December 31, 1986, both published by Lipper Analytical Services, Inc.

TABLE C
Selected Larger Tax-Exempt Bond Funds (a)

Name	5-Year Total Return (b)	Minimum Initial Investment	Telephone Number
NO-LOAD FUNDS			
Dreyfus Tax-Exempt Bond Fund	137%	$2,500	800-645-6561
Federated Tax-Free Income Fund	143	500	800-245-4770
Fidelity Municipal Bond Portfolio	139	2,500	800-544-6666
Financial Tax-Free Income Shares	135	250	800-525-8085
SAFECO Municipal Bond Fund	148	2,500	800-426-6730
SteinRoe Managed Municipals	170	2,500	800-621-0320
Vanguard Municipal Bond Fund (Long-Term Portfolio)	138	3,000	800-662-7447
LOAD FUNDS			
American Capital Municipal Bond Fund	150	500	800-231-3638
IDS Tax-Exempt Bond Fund	150	2,000	800-328-8300
Kemper Municipal Bond Fund	157	1,000	800-621-1148
MFS Managed Municipal Bond Trust	152	250	800-343-2829
New England Tax-Exempt Income Fund	159	250	800-343-7104
Oppenheimer Tax-Free Bond Fund	170	1,000	800-525-7048
Putnam Tax-Exempt Income Fund	167	500	800-225-1581
United Municipal Bond Fund	146	500	800-821-5664

(a) No 10-year performance records are shown because tax-exempt bond funds first were permitted in 1976, and accordingly very few of the funds have 10-year records. The period 1982–1986 was generally one of declining interest rates and rising bond prices; the high rates of return achieved over that period are not likely to be equalled in most future periods, and should not be taken as an indication of future results.

(b) Percent increase in value of an investment over the five years 1982–1986, assuming all income dividends and capital gains distributions reinvested, and without any deduction for any commission (load) paid.

Note: Total return statistics derived from data published in *Lipper—Fixed Income Fund Performance Analysis*, December 31, 1986, published by Lipper Analytical Services, Inc.

TABLE D

Selected Major No-Load Mutual Fund Groups

Name of Group or Manager	Toll-free Telephone Number
Dreyfus Funds (b)	800-645-6561
Fidelity Group (a)	800-544-6666
Financial Programs	800-525-8085
Neuberger & Berman Management	800-367-0770
T. Rowe Price Funds	800-638-5660
Scudder Funds	800-225-2470
SteinRoe & Farnham Funds	800-621-0320
Twentieth Century Funds (a)	800-345-2021
USAA Investment Management	800-531-8000
Value Line Group	800-223-0818
Vanguard Group	800-662-7447

(a) Group also includes one or more low-load funds.
(b) Group also includes load and low-load funds.

INDEX

ABOUT THE AUTHORS

ARNOLD CORRIGAN, noted financial expert, is the author of *How Your IRA Can Make You a Millionaire* and is a frequent guest on financial talk shows. A senior officer of a large New York investment advisory firm, he holds Bachelor's and Master's degrees in economics from Harvard and has written for *Barron's* and other financial publications.

PHYLLIS C. KAUFMAN, the originator of the *No Nonsense Guides*, is a Philadelphia attorney and theatrical producer. A graduate of Brandeis University, she was an editor of the law review at Temple University School of Law. She is listed in *Who's Who in American Law, Who's Who of American Women, Who's Who in Finance and Industry,* and *Foremost Women of the Twentieth Century.*